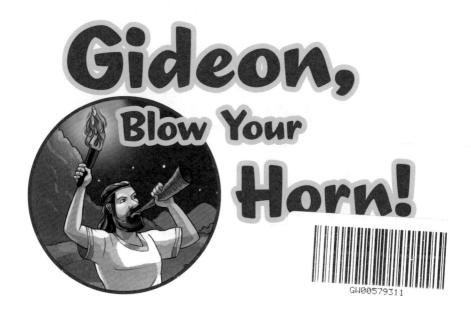

Written by Jennifer Nystrom and Marjorie Redford

Illustrated by Bill Dickson

*Based on Judges 7:1-21*

*Gideon, Blow Your Horn!* copyright © 2009 by Tyndale House Publishers, Inc., Carol Stream, Illinois 60188. All rights reserved. www.tyndale.com. Originally published by Standard Publishing, Cincinnati, Ohio. First printing by Tyndale House Publishers, Inc., in 2015. Cover design: Andrew Quach. *TYNDALE*, Tyndale's quill logo, and *Happy Day* are registered trademarks of Tyndale House Publishers, Inc. All rights reserved. For manufacturing information regarding this product, please call 1-800-323-9400.

ISBN 978-1-4964-1112-9

Printed in the United States of America

| 21 | 20 | 19 | 18 | 17 | 16 | 15 |
|----|----|----|----|----|----|----|
| 7  | 6  | 5  | 4  | 3  | 2  | 1  |

*Tyndale House Publishers, Inc.*
*Carol Stream, Illinois*

Long ago God chose a man named Gideon to be the leader of the Israelites, God's people. Gideon loved God. He listened to God to know how to lead his people.

The Midianites were ruling over God's people. The
Midianites did not worship God, and they did not like the
Israelites. God wanted Gideon to lead his people against
the Midianites. So Gideon called together a big army. Was it
time to go to the camp of Midian?

No. God said there were too many men in Gideon's army. Too many men? Yes, too many men!

"If any of you are afraid, you may go home," Gideon said. And many of the men chose to leave. Was it time to go now?

Not yet. God said there were *still* too many men. Gideon listened as God told him how to choose his army. By the time Gideon was done, there were only 300 men left—but they were God's 300 men.

That night, God told Gideon to take one of his helpers and go down to the camp of the Midianite army. God said, "I will help you not be afraid." So Gideon and his helper quietly crept down to where they could see the army of the Midianites.

Gideon and his helper were surprised at what they
saw. There were men and camels everywhere! There
were so many men and camels that they could not count
them all.

How could Gideon and his small army of 300 men
defeat all of these people?

Then Gideon overheard two men talking. They were talking about a dream. The dream meant God was going to help Gideon defeat the army of Midian.

When Gideon heard this, he worshiped and thanked God. Then Gideon and his helper hurried back to the camp of Israel. Was it time to go now?

Yes! Gideon said, "Get up! God is going to help us. Follow me. Do what I do."

Gideon quickly split his men into three groups. Every
man had a trumpet and a torch hidden inside a big jar.
Gideon led the men to the camp of Midian. Everything
was just the way God wanted it to be. *Gideon, blow
your horn!*

Gideon blew his horn and broke his jar. All of his men blew their horns and broke their jars. They shouted, "For the Lord and for Gideon!" The jars crashed loudly. The torches lit up the night sky. The trumpets woke the sleeping army of Midian.

The Midianite soldiers were so confused by all the lights and loud noises that they began to fight each other. Soon Gideon's army had defeated the army of Midian.

Was it the right time to go? Yes! Gideon had listened to God. Gideon was a good leader for God's people.